WICKED
COCKNEY
RHYMING SLANG

Betty Kirkpatrick

10652998

First published in Great Britain in 2002 by
Michael O'Mara Books Limited
9 Lion Yard
Tremadoc Road
London SW4 7NQ

The material in this compilation first appeared in
The Little Book of Cockney Rhyming Slang by Betty Kirkpatrick copyright
© 2001 Michael O'Mara Books Ltd.

A CIP catalogue record for this book is available from
the British Library

ISBN 1-85479-386-1

1 3 5 7 9 10 8 6 4 2

Designed and typeset by Design 23

Printed and bound by Bookmarque Limited, UK

INTRODUCTION

Cockney rhyming slang is a variety of idiomatic speech in which a particular word is replaced with a phrase of two or three words which rhymes with it. The slang originated in London and some of the rhymes are true rhymes only if they are sounded in line with Cockney pronunciation.

This form of slang is almost certainly not as old as we might assume, the likelihood being that it came into existence at the beginning of the twentieth century. It should be remembered, however, that ascribing precise dates to language can be very difficult, particularly language like rhyming slang, which was originally handed on by word of mouth.

The reason for the rise of Cockney rhyming slang is not all that clear either, but there is a distinct possibility that it came into being as a means of keeping the police ignorant of what was happening around them. Thus rhyming slang might well have been originally a kind of code used by criminal groups, such as vagabonds, thieves and the less honest street sellers, to pass on secret information to each other.

There is an element of humour and ingenuity about

much rhyming slang and so it was gradually taken up by other people, originally members of the working classes, who had not necessarily anything to hide from the police. It even left the confines of London with people who emigrated from there, and made its way to Australia and America.

Sometimes the slang was, and is, used as a kind of euphemism for words relating to subjects that might cause embarrassment – bodily functions, for example. The rhymes often refer to people who are or were topical at the time the rhyming phrase was coined, and not infrequently the phrase outlasts their popularity. Thus rhyming slang easily becomes obscure.

Nevertheless, rhyming slang has not only survived the decades, but it is currently enjoying something of a revival; a revival seemingly helped by the Internet. This is particularly true among young people who may feel attracted to its inventiveness and its irreverence. Cockney rhyming slang tends to be at the opposite end of the spectrum from politically correct language.

This book gives a selection of examples of Cockney rhyming slang, both old and new. My apologies if your own particular favourite is missing. Still, it's worth a butcher's hook.

RHYMING SLANG to ENGLISH

Aa

Abergavenny a penny

Abraham Lincoln stinking

Adam and Eve believe

Alan Whickers knickers (Alan Whicker
[b. 1925], British TV personality)

airs and graces **1** faces **2** braces
3 horse races

apples, apples and pears stairs

apple tart a fart

Aristotle a bottle

artful dodger lodger (a character in *Oliver Twist*
[1839], a novel by Charles Dickens [1812-70])

Arthur Rank **1** bank (financial) **2** act of
masturbation (vulgar slang **wank**) (J. Arthur,
Lord Rank [1888-1972], British film magnate)

Auntie Ella umbrella

Auntie Nellie stomach (informal **belly**)

Ayrton Senna ten pounds sterling (informal **tenner**) (Brazilian racing driver [1960-94])

Bb

babbling brook crook, criminal

baby's pram jam

backseat driver lazy person (slang **skiver**)

bacon and eggs legs

bacon rind blind

Baden-Powell trowel (Robert, Lord Baden-Powell [1857-1941], soldier, founder of the Scout movement)

bag of flour shower (of rain)

bag of fruit a suit

bag of yeast priest

baker's dozen cousin

ball and bat hat

ball of chalk **1** a walk **2** a talk

ball of lead head

Band of Hope soap (a British temperance society formed in 1847)

bangers and mash **1** act of urinating (vulgar slang **slash**) **2** cash

Barnaby Rudge a judge (a character in the novel of the same name [1841] by Charles Dickens [1812-70])

barnet, Barnet Fair hair (a major horse fair held in Barnet, Greater London, from the sixteenth to the eighteenth centuries)

bar of soap cannabis (slang **dope**)

bat and wicket ticket

bath bun **1** son **2** the sun

battle cruiser pub (slang **boozer**)

bazaar bar (drinking establishment)

bees and honey money

beg your pardon a garden

bell-ringers fingers

bended knees cheese

Benny Hill **1** drill **2** till (cash) (British comedian
[1925-92])

berk, Berkeley Hunt stupid, foolish or
annoying person (vulgar slang **cunt**)

Bernie Flint penniless (slang **skint**)

Betty Grable table (US film star [1916-73])

Bexleyheath teeth (town in Greater London)

Big Ben 1 ten **2** ten pounds sterling

big bloke cocaine (slang **coke**)

big dippers slippers

Billy Bunter ordinary person, customer, someone who bets (slang **punter**) (a large and foolish schoolboy, the principal character in the 'Greyfriars' novels of Frank Richards [1876-1961])

billy goat a coat

Billy Liar tyre (the title of a novel [1959] by Keith Waterhouse [b. 1929], later filmed)

bird, birdlime prison sentence (slang **time**)

biscuits and cheese knees

Black & Decker penis (vulgar slang **pecker**) (the trade name of a manufacturer of power tools)

blindman's buff snuff (tobacco)

blue moon a spoon

board and plank an American (slang **Yank**)

boat and oar prostitute (**whore**)

bob and dick **1** sick **2** penis (vulgar slang **dick, prick, wick**)

Bob Hope cannabis (slang **dope**) (US comedian and film star [b. 1903])

booed and hissed drunk (vulgar slang **pissed**)

boots and socks venereal disease (informal **pox**)

bo peep **1** sleep **2** a peep (glimpse, look) (from the nursery rhyme 'Little Bo Peep')

boracic, boracic lint penniless (slang **skint**)

born and bred bed

borrow and beg egg

bottle nerve, courage (from **bottle and glass**, vulgar slang **arse,** since someone who is terrified is thought likely to foul himself; hence **to lose one's bottle** means to give way to nerves or fear)

bottle and stopper police officer (slang **copper**)

bottle of beer ear

bottle of porter daughter

bottle of sauce a horse

bottle of scent effeminate, homosexual (slang **bent**)

bottle of water daughter

bottle of wine a fine (penalty)

bow and arrow **1** sparrow **2** barrow **3** charabanc (informal **chara**)

bow and quiver liver

Brahms and Liszt drunk (vulgar slang **pissed**) (the composers [German and Hungarian, respectively] Johannes Brahms [1833-97] and Franz Liszt [1811-86])

brandy snap a slap

brass band hand

brass tacks facts

brave and bold cold

bread and cheese a sneeze

bread and honey money

bread and lard hard

bread knife wife

Brenda Frickers knickers (Brenda Fricker, [b. 1944] Irish actress)

Brian Clough rough (British football manager [b. 1935])

Brian O'Flynn gin

bricks and mortar daughter

Brighton Pier 1 queer **2** to disappear, leave or run away

Brighton rock the dock (in a courtroom)

Bristol, Bristol city female breast (vulgar slang **titty**)

British Rail e-mail

Britney Spears beers (US pop singer [b. 1981])

broken heart a fart

broken quiver liver

brother and sister a blister

Brown Bess yes (British military musket used during the Napoleonic Wars)

brown bread dead

Brown Joe no

Brussels sprout Boy Scout

bubble and squeak **1** a Greek **2** week **3** act of urinating (vulgar slang **leak**)

bubble bath a laugh

bubble gum buttocks (informal **bum**)

Bugs Bunny money (a Warner Brothers cartoon-film character, created in 1940)

bull and cow row (quarrel, argument)

Bunsen burner profit-making scheme (informal **earner**)

burglar alarm arm

Burlington Bertie thirty ('Burlington Bertie from Bow', a popular song [1915] by W. F. Hargreaves [1846-1919])

burnt cinder window

Burton-on-Trent rent

bushel and peck neck

Buster Keaton meeting (US silent-film comedian [1895-1966])

butcher's, butcher's hook a look, glance

buttered bread dead

buttered bun one (number)

buttons and bows toes

Cc

cab rank bank (financial)

Cain and Abel table

Calcutta butter

Calvin Klein 1 fine (penalty) **2** wine
  3 nine (US fashion designer [b. 1942])

canal boat the tote (state betting system)

can of Coke a joke

can of oil a boil (spot)

Captain Bligh a pie (William Bligh [*c.* 1753-1817], captain of HMS *Bounty*, the crew of which mutinied in 1789)

Captain Cook **1** a look **2** a book (James Cook [1728-79], British navigator and explorer)

captain's log toilet (slang **bog**)

cardboard box venereal disease (informal **pox**)

car park police informer (slang **nark**)

carving knife wife

cash and carried married

cat and mouse a house

Cecil Gee knee (chain of menswear shops)

chain and locket a pocket

Charing Cross horse

chalfonts haemorrhoids (informal **piles**) (Chalfont St Giles, village in Buckinghamshire)

Charles Dance a chance (British film, TV and stage actor [b. 1946])

Charles James **1** theatre box **2** a fox (Charles James Fox [1749-1806], British Whig politician, statesman and orator)

Charley Frisky whisky

Charley Howard coward

Charley Mason **1** basin **2** basinful (i.e. a great deal; too much of)

Charley Randy brandy

Charley Skinner dinner

Charlie Drake **1** a break, free time **2** vehicle brake (British comedian [b. 1925])

Charlie Prescott waistcoat

Charlie Pride a ride (on horseback, in a car etc.)

Charlie Ronce a pimp (slang **ponce**)

Charlie Smirke stupid or foolish person (vulgar rhyming slang **berk** [q.v.])

charming wife a knife

Chatham and Dover to stop doing something (slang **give over**) (towns in Kent)

cheese and crackers testicles (vulgar slang **knackers**)

cheese and rice Jesus Christ (as an oath)

cheese grater waiter

Cheesey Quaver a favour (trade name of a kind of savoury snack)

Chelsea bun **1** son **2** the sun

Cheltenham gold cold (Cheltenham Gold Cup, a National Hunt race meeting)

cherrypicker one pound sterling (slang **nicker**)

cherry red head

Chevy Chase face (sixteenth-century English ballad about a Border battle between Scots and English)

chicken and rice nice

chicken's neck cheque

china, china plate friend (informal **mate**)

chips and peas knees

chopping sticks six

chorus and verse buttocks, anus (vulgar slang **arse**)

Christmas crackered exhausted (slang **knackered**)

Christmas Eve believe

Christopher Lee act of urinating (informal **pee**) (British film actor [b. 1922])

Cilla Black the back (British singer and TV personality [b. 1943])

Claire Rayner trainer (shoe) (British agony aunt and novelist [b. 1931]

Clark Kent corrupt (slang **bent**) (the pseudonym of the comic-strip character Superman in his ordinary life)

clever Mike bicycle (**bike**)

clickety-click sixty-six

clothes pegs legs

club and stick detective (US slang **dick**)

coat and badge to cadge

cobblers, cobbler's awls **1** testicles (vulgar slang **balls**) **2** nonsense, rubbish

cob o'coal dole (unemployment benefit)

cock and hen, cockle and hen **1** ten **2** ten pounds

cock linnet a minute (time)

cod's roe money (slang **dough**)

cold potato waiter

collar and tie a lie (untruth)

Colonel Gaddafi café (Moamar Muhammad al-Gaddafi [b. 1942], Libyan leader [1969-])

comb and brush alcoholic drink, an alcoholic (slang **lush**)

Conan Doyle a boil (spot) (Sir Arthur Conan Doyle [1859-1930], novelist and creator of Sherlock Holmes)

conger eel tell on, inform (on someone to) a person in authority (slang **squeal**)

constant screamer concertina

corned beef **1** thief **2** chief prison officer

corns and bunions onions

cough and choke to smoke (cigarettes etc.)

cough and sneeze cheese

cough and stutter butter

country cousin dozen

cow and calf **1** a laugh **2** half

cow's lick prison (slang **nick**)

cream cookie bookmaker (slang **bookie**)

cream crackered exhausted (slang **knackered**)

cream puff bad temper (**huff**)

Crimea beer (from the Crimean War [1853-6], in which Britain, France, Turkey and Sardinia fought Russia)

crowded space suitcase

crown jewels tools

crust of bread head

currant bread dead

currant bun **1** son **2** the sun

custard and jelly television (informal **telly**)

Dd

daft and barmy army

daily bread head (of the family)

daisy beat to cheat, swindle

daisy roots boots

Damon Hill pill (British racing driver
    [b. 1960])

dancing fleas keys

Danny La Rue clue, idea (the stage name of
    British entertainer and female impersonator
    Daniel Patrick Carroll
    [b. 1927])

Darby and Joan 1 telephone (**phone**)
    2 alone (idealized elderly couple, from an
    eighteenth-century English ballad)

Darby Kelly stomach (informal **belly**)

Darren Gough a cough (English cricketer [b. 1970])

David Gower shower (of rain) (English cricketer [b. 1957])

Davy Crockett a pocket (US lawyer, politician, frontiersman and soldier [1786-1836])

dead horse tomato sauce

deep-sea diver five pounds sterling (informal **fiver**)

Desmond a lower-second (informal **'Two-two'**) university degree (Desmond Tutu [b. 1931], South African clergyman and political activist)

deuce and ace face

dicky-bird word

didn't ought port (wine)

didn't oughter water

dig a grave to shave

dirty daughter water

do as you like a bicycle (**bike**)

doctor and nurse purse

Doctor Crippen dripping (fat) (Dr Hawley Harvey Crippen [1862-1910], US-born British murderer)

dog and bone telephone (**phone**)

dog's, dog's meat feet

Dolly Cotton rotten

dolly mixtures cinema (the **pictures**) (small, coloured sweets sold as a mixture)

Dolly Varden a garden (a character in the novel *Barnaby Rudge* [1841] by Charles Dickens [1812-70])

Donald Trump bowel movement (vulgar slang **dump**) (US property developer [b. 1946])

don't make a fuss bus

door-to-door four

dot and carry marry

dot and dash cash

Douglas Hurd 1 lump of excrement (vulgar
slang **turd**) **2** third-class university degree
(**Third**) (Douglas, Lord Hurd [b. 1930], British
Conservative politician)

down the drain brain

D'Oyly Carte a fart (Richard D'Oyly Carte
[1844-1901], impresario, founder [1875] of an
opera company noted for its performances of
the works of Gilbert and Sullivan)

dripping toast publican (informal/facetious
mine host)

drum and bass home (**place**)

drum and fife 1 a knife **2** wife

Dublin trick a brick

Duchess of Fife wife

Duke of Kent **1** rent **2** homosexual (slang **bent**)

Duke of York **1** fork **2** talk **3** chalk (for billiards and snooker cues) **4** walk **5** pork

Dunlop tyre liar

dustbin lid child (informal **kid**)

Dutch pegs legs

Dutch, Dutch plate friend (informal **mate**)

early bird word

Eartha Kitt bowel movement (vulgar slang **shit**) (US singer and actress [b. 1928])

earwig understand (slang **twig**)

east and south mouth

east and west vest

Easter bunny money

Easter egg leg

eau de cologne telephone (**phone**)

egg yoke a joke

Eiffel Tower shower (of rain)

Elephant and Castle anus (vulgar slang **arsehole**) (district in South London; the name is said to derive from a visit of the Infanta of Castile)

elephant's trunk drunk

Epsom races **1** braces **2** faces

Errol Flynn chin (Australian-born film star [1909-59])

Ff

false alarm arm

Farmer Giles haemorrhoids (informal **piles**)

fiddle and flute a suit

fife and drum buttocks (informal **bum**)

fine and dandy brandy

finger and thumb 1 rum 2 keep quiet
(informal **mum**) 3 friend (informal **chum**)
4 a drum

fisherman's daughter water

flea and louse 1 house 2 brothel (informal
house [of ill repute])

fleas and ants trousers, pants

flounder and dab taxi (**cab**)

flowery dell prison cell

fly-by-nights tights

flying trapeze cheese

fly-tipper child (informal **nipper**)

fore and aft daft

fork and knife **1** wife **2** life

Fortnum and Mason **1** basin **2** pudding basin
(famous store in Central London, noted for its
food department)

forty-four **1** prostitute (**whore**) **2** door-to-door
salesman

France and Spain rain

Frank Bough stale, rotting (informal **off**) (British
sports commentator [b. 1933])

fridge freezer person, man (slang **geezer**)

frisk and frolic soap (originally **carbolic** soap)

frock and frill a chill

frog and toad road

frog in the throat boat

fun and frolics testicles (vulgar slang **bollocks**)

garden gate **1** friend (informal **mate**)
2 magistrate **3** eight

garden gnome a comb

garden plant aunt

Gary Glitter **1** pint of bitter (beer) **2** anus
(vulgar slang **shitter**) (stage name of British
pop singer Paul Gadd [b. 1940])

gay and frisky whisky

gay and hearty a party

Gay Gordon traffic warden

general election erection

Geoff Hurst 1 first-class university degree (**First**)
   2 a thirst **3** burst (English footballer [b. 1941])

Gert and Daisy lazy (characters in a radio show
   created by British comediennes Elsie and Doris
   Waters in the 1930s)

giggle and titter pint of bitter (beer)

ginger ale gaol

ginger beer 1 queer (strange)
   2 homosexual (informal **queer**)

ginger pop police officer (slang **cop**)

giraffe laugh

give and get a bet

glass of beer ear

Glenn Hoddle something simple (informal **doddle**) (British football manager and former player [b. 1957])

glory be tea

God forbid **1** child (informal **kid**) **2** hat (informal **lid**)

God in heaven seven

gold watch Scotch (whisky)

gone to bed dead

goose and duck sexual intercourse (vulgar slang **fuck**)

goose's neck cheque

grease and grime time

greengages wages

Gregory Peck **1** neck **2** cheque (US film star [b. 1916])

grey mare a fare (bus, train, etc.)

grumble and mutter a bet (informal **flutter**)

guinea pig wig

Gypsy Rose Lee tea (stage name of the US actress, striptease artiste and author Rose Louise Hovick [1914-70])

gypsy's kiss act of urinating (vulgar slang **piss**)

Hh

haddock and bloater car (informal **motor**)

hair gel bell

hairy knees please

hale and hearty party

half-inch steal (informal **pinch**)

ham and bone **1** home **2** telephone (informal **phone**)

ham and cheesy easy

hammer and discus whiskers (beard etc.)
Hampstead Heath teeth (area of park and
  woodland in North London)

hampton, Hampton Wick penis (vulgar slang
  prick) (village in Greater London)

ham shank an American (slang **Yank**)

hand and fist drunk (vulgar slang **pissed**)

Hank Marvin starving (British pop guitarist [b.
  1941])

happy hour **1** flower **2** shower (of rain)

harbour light all right

hard and flat a hat

hare and hound round (of drinks)

Harold Macmillan villain (1st Earl of Stockton
  [1894-1986], British Conservative politician;
  Prime Minister [1957-63])

Harry Tate **1** late **2** plate **3** eight (British stage comedian [1872-1940])

Harvey Nichols pickles (well-known Central London department store)

hat and scarf a bath

haystack the back

heart of oak penniless (slang **broke**)

heaven and hell smell

heavens above love

Henrietta a letter

here and there chair

herring and kipper striptease artiste (**stripper**)

hide and seek cheek (impertinence)

Highland fling **1** string **2** a ring **3** sing

high seas knees

high-stepper pepper

hit and miss **1** a kiss **2** urine (vulgar slang **piss**)

hit and run the sun

Holy Ghost **1** the post (mail) **2** the starting or winning post on a racecourse **3** toast

Hong Kong **1** wrong **2** a smell (slang **pong**)

horn of plenty twenty

horse and cart **1** heart **2** a fart

hot and cold gold

hot dinner a winner

hot toddy the body

House of Fraser razor (chain of department stores)

house to let a bet

Howard's Way gay, homosexual (TV serial of the 1980s)

hugs and kisses wife (informal **missus**)

hurricane lamp a tramp

husband and wife a knife

Hush Puppy a yuppie (the trade name of a
   brand of shoes)

Hyde Park police informer (slang **nark**) (large
   park in Central London)

ice-cream freezer man, person (slang **geezer**)

ideal home a comb

inky blue influenza (**flu**)

insects and ants trousers (**pants**)

inside right mean (informal **tight**)

in the mood food

in the nude food

Irish jig wig

Irish stew true

iron girder murder

Iron Mike bicycle (**bike**)

iron tank bank (financial)

Isle of Wight **1** right, all right **2** light
    3 mean (informal **tight**)

itch and scratch a match (light)

ivory pearl girl

Jj

Jack and Jill **1** hill **2** pill **3** till (cash)

Jackanory story (children's TV series in which stories were read aloud)

Jack Jones, on one's alone, on one's own

jack of spades sunglasses (slang **shades**)

Jack's alive five

Jackson Pollocks testicles (vulgar slang **bollocks**) (US artist [1912-56])

jack tar bar (drinking establishment)

jack the lad bad

Jack the Ripper **1** kipper **2** slipper (name given to a British serial murderer, never identified, who killed and mutilated at least seven prostitutes in London's East End [August-November 1888])

Jagger's lips chips (Mick Jagger [b. 1943], British rock star)

jam jar car

jam roll **1** parole **2** dole (unemployment benefit)

jar of jam **1** pram **2** tram

Jasper Carrott a parrot (British comedian [b. 1945])

jellied eels transport, especially a car (informal **wheels**)

Jennie Lee **1** tea **2** key **3** flea (Baroness Lee of Asheridge [1904-88], Scottish Labour politician, wife of Aneurin Bevan [1897-1960])

Jenny Lind wind (flatulence) (Swedish soprano [1820-87])

Jeremiah a fire

Jimmy Hill a pill (British football commentator [b. 1928])

Jimmy Nail 1 stale 2 a sale 3 mail (British actor and singer [b. 1954])

Jimmy Riddle act of urinating (informal **piddle**)

Jimmy Skinner dinner

Jimmy Young 1 tongue 2 bribe (slang **bung**) (British singer and radio presenter [b. 1923])

Joanna piano

jockey's whip 1 sleep (slang **kip**) 2 chip (potato)

Jodrell Bank act of masturbation (vulgar slang **wank**)

Joe Baxi taxi

Joe Blake 1 steak 2 snake

Joe Brown town (British pop singer and actor [b. 1941])

Joe McBride sexual intercourse (slang **ride**)

Joe Roke a cigarette break (informal **smoke**)

Joe Soap a fool (informal **dope**)

John Cleese cheese (British actor and comedian
   [b. 1939])

John Major a wager (British Conservative
   politician [b. 1943]; Prime Minister
   [1990-7])

Johnnie Walker talker, informer (popular brand
   of whisky)

John Wayne train (stage name of Marion
   Michael Morrison, US film star [1907-79])

Jolly Roger lodger

joy of my life wife

Judi Dench stench (Dame Judi Dench, British
   actress and stage director [b. 1934])

jug and pail gaol

Julian Clary a male homosexual (slang **fairy**)
   (British entertainer [b. 1959])

Kk

Kate Carney army (British music-hall star [1869-1950])

Ken Dodd roll of banknotes (informal **wad**) (British comedian and singer [b. 1931])

kick and prance a dance

King Canutes boots (Canute [Cnut] [*c.* 955-1035], Danish king of England [1016-35], Denmark [1018-35] and Norway [1028-35], who supposedly tried to hold back the tide)

King Death bad breath

kingdom come **1** rum **2** buttocks (informal **bum**)

King Lear **1** ear **2** homosexual (informal **queer**) (from the play [*c.* 1605] by William Shakespeare [1564-1616])

kings and queens baked beans

kipper and plaice face

kiss and cuddle a muddle

kiss of life wife

kitchen sink a drink (alcoholic)

knobbly knee key

knock at the door four

knocker and knob job

kung-fu fighter cigarette lighter

la-di-dah 1 cigar 2 car

Lady Godiva 1 five 2 five pounds (informal **fiver**) ([?1040-80] wife of Leofric, Earl of Mercia; said to have ridden naked through

Coventry to persuade her husband to lift taxes imposed on the townspeople)

Lambeth Walk chalk (for billiards and snooker cues) (dance – and song – popularized by the musical *Me and My Gal* [1932]; from the name of a street in Lambeth, South London)

lame duck sexual intercourse (vulgar slang **fuck**)

lath and plaster employer (**master**)

laugh and joke a cigarette break (informal **smoke**)

laugh and titter a pint of bitter (beer)

lean and fat a hat

Lee Marvin very hungry (**starving**) (US film star [1924-87])

left and right a fight

leg of beef thief

lemon curd **1** lump of excrement (vulgar slang **turd**) **2** girl, young woman (slang **bird**)

Len Hutton button (Sir Leonard Hutton, English cricketer [1916-90])

Leslie Ash, go for a urinate (vulgar slang **go for a slash**) (British actress [b. 1960])

Lester Piggott bigot (British flat-racing jockey [b. 1935])

life and death breath

Lillian Gish **1** dish **2** fish **3** urine (vulgar slang **pish**) (stage name of Lillian de Guiche, US film and stage actress [1899-1993])

Lionel Bart a fart (British composer and playwright [1930-99])

Lionel Blair **1** chair **2** mare (British entertainer [b. 1931])

Lionel Blairs flared trousers (informal **flares**) (see preceding entry)

lion's roar a snore

little and large margarine (informal **marge**)

Little Peter meter (for gas, electricity, etc.)

loaf, loaf of bread head

London fog dog

loop the loop soup

lord and mastered drunk (slang **plastered**)

lord mayor to swear (curse)

Lorna Doone spoon (the heroine of a novel [1869] of the same name by R. D. Blackmore [1825-1900])

love and kisses wife (informal **missus**)

lucky charm arm

lump and bump fool (informal **chump**)

lump of ice advice

Mm

macaroni twenty-five pounds sterling (slang
pony)

Mae West female breast (US film star [1892-
1980])

Mahatma Gandhi **1** brandy **2** shandy
3 randy (Mohandas Karamchand Gandhi,
Indian social reformer and spiritual and
political leader [1869-1948])

man alive five

man and wife a knife

marbles and conkers mad, crazy (slang
bonkers)

Mars and Venus penis

Mars Bar a scar

Maud and Ruth truth

Max Walls testicles (vulgar slang **balls**) (Max Wall, British comedian [1908-90])

Melvyn Bragg sexual intercourse (vulgar slang **shag**) (Melvyn, Lord Bragg, British novelist and TV presenter [b. 1939])

merchant banker masturbator (slang **wanker**), used as a general term of abuse

merry old soul 1 coal **2** a hole

Michael Caine 1 pain **2** stain (Sir Michael Caine, British film actor [b. 1933])

Michael Winner dinner (British film director and restaurant critic [b. 1935])

Mike Malone telephone (**phone**)

Milky Way homosexual (informal **gay**)

miller's daughter water

minces, mince pies eyes

moan and wail gaol

Moby Dick sick (the white whale in the novel [1851] of the same name by US writer Herman Melville [1819-91])

Molly McGuire a fire

monkey's cousin twelve (a **dozen**)

more or less a dress

Mother Hubbard cupboard

Mother Kelly **1** jelly **2** television (informal **telly**)

Mutt and Jeff deaf (US cartoon characters created by H. C. 'Bud' Fischer in the 1930s)

mutter and stutter butter

Mystic Meg leg (British popular astrologer formerly involved in the broadcasting of the National Lottery results)

Nn

Nancy Lee **1** tea **2** flea

nanny goat **1** a coat **2** boat **3** throat
4 the tote (state betting system)

Nat King Cole the dole (unemployment benefit)
(US popular singer [1919-65])

needle and pin **1** gin **2** thin

needle and thread bread

needles and pins twins

Nelson Eddies cash (slang **the readies**) (Nelson
Eddy, US popular singer [1901-67])

nervous wreck cheque

never fear pint of beer

Niagara Falls testicles (vulgar slang **balls**)

night and day a play (drama)

Noah's ark **1** lark (prank) **2** lark (bird)
    3 park **4** informer (slang **nark**) **5** shark

Nobby Stiles haemorrhoids (informal **piles**)
    (British footballer [b. 1942])

north and south mouth

nose and chin **1** gin **2** a win (on a wager)

now and never clever

nuclear sub pub

Nuremberg trials haemorrhoids (informal
    piles) (trials of the principal leaders of Nazi
    Germany for war crimes at Nuremberg [1945-6])

Oo

ocean pearl girl

ocean wave a shave

Oedipus Rex sex (character in Greek mythology who, unaware of their relationship to him, kills his father and marries his mother)

oily rag cigarette (slang **fag**)

old fogey snot (vulgar slang **bogey**)

Old King Cole dole (unemployment benefit)

old nag cigarette (slang **fag**)

old pot and pan husband (**man**)

Oliver Twist drunk (vulgar slang **pissed**) (hero of the novel [1839] of the same name by Charles Dickens [1812-70])

on and off a cough

one another **1** mother **2** brother

open the door four

orchestra stalls testicles (vulgar slang **balls**)

Orinoco **1** cocoa **2** a poker (a river in Venezuela and Colombia)

Orphan Annie vagina (vulgar slang **fanny**)

over the stile committed for trial

Oxford bag cigarette (slang **fag**) (Oxford bags, trousers with very loose baggy legs, first popular in the 1920s)

Oxo cube the London Underground (informal **Tube**) (trade name of a kind of condensed stock sold in cubes for use in cooking)

Pp

pain in the neck cheque

paper bag to nag

paper hat fool (slang **prat**)

paraffin lamp a tramp

Pat and Mick sick

Pat Cash act of urinating (vulgar slang **slash**)
   (Australian champion tennis player [b. 1965]))

peace and quiet a diet

pearly gate plate

Peckham Rye tie (neckwear) (district in Greater
   London)

pen and ink a stink

penny black the back

penny locket pocket

Peter Pan 1 a tan 2 a van (chief character in
the play [1904] of the same name by
J. M. [Sir James] Barrie [1860-1937])

Petticoat Lane pain (street and street market in
East London)

philharmonic gin and tonic

Piccadilly silly

pick and choose alcohol, an alcoholic drink
(slang **booze**)

pick up sticks six

pie and liquor vicar

pie and mash 1 cash 2 act of urinating (vulgar
slang **slash**) 3 showy (slang **flash**)

pig's ear beer

pig's trotter a squatter

pillar and post ghost

pink lint penniless (slang **skint**)

plate and dish a wish

plates, plates of meat feet

Plymouth Argyll file (tool) (English football
  team)

poor relation station (railway)

pork chop police officer (slang **cop**)

port and brandy randy

pot and pan man, husband

pot of glue **1** clue **2** queue

pot of honey money

potted head dead

pound note a coat

pound of lead head

pounds and pence sense

pudding chef deaf

puddings and pies eyes

puff and drag a cigarette (slang **fag**)

Punch and Judy moody

Queen's Park Rangers strangers (English football team)

Rr

rabbit hutch groin (**crotch**)

rain and pour to snore

Ramsgate Sands hands (the seaside resort, Ramsgate, Kent)

Raquel Welch a belch (US film star [b. 1940])

raspberry ripple nipple

raspberry tart a fart

rat and mouse a house

rattle and clank bank (financial)

rattle and jar car

read and write **1** to fight **2** escape (**flight**)

reeling and rocking stocking

rhythm and blues shoes

ribbon and curl girl (child)

rifle range change (money)

rip and tear to swear

rising damp cramp

River Ouse alcohol, an alcoholic drink (slang **booze**) (name of several English rivers)

River Tyne wine (a river in north-east England)

roast beef teeth

roast pork a fork

Robin Hood good

rock'n'roll dole (unemployment benefit)

rock of ages wages

rocks and boulders shoulders

roller coaster toaster

rolling billow a pillow

Ronnie Biggs lodgings (informal **digs**) (English
   criminal, one of the Great Train   Robbers
   of 1963, recently returned to finish his prison
   sentence in Britain [b. 1929])

roof rack back

Rory O'Moore **1** floor **2** door **3** prostitute
   (**whore**)

rosie, Rosie Lee tea

Rosie O'Grady's women's toilet (**ladies'**)

round and square everywhere

round the houses trousers

Royal Mail bail

Royal Navy gravy

rub-a-dub a pub

rubber duck sexual intercourse (vulgar slang
  fuck)

Ruby Murray a curry (British popular singer
  [1935-96])

ruby red head

runner and rider cider

rusty nail gaol

Ss

sad and sorry lorry

safe and sound the ground

saint and sinner dinner

salmon and trout **1** tobacco (slang **snout**)
  2 nose (informal **snout**) **3** stout (beer)
  4 tout **5** gout

Santa's grotto drunk (slang **blotto**)

satin and silk milk

saucepan lid a child (informal **kid**)

sausage and mash **1** cash **2** car crash

sausage roll the dole (unemployment benefit)

scarper, Scapa Flow to run away, get
   out (**go**) (British naval anchorage in the Orkney
   Islands, used in both world wars)

Scotch eggs legs

Sebastian Coe toe (British athlete and politician
   [b. 1956])

seek and search church

Sexton Blake a fake (fictional detective created
   by Edwy Searles Brooks (1889-1965) in 1912)

Sharon Stone a telephone (**phone**)
   (US film star [b. 1957])

shepherd's pie the sky

Sherman tank an American (slang **Yank**) (main battle tank of the Allies during the Second World War; US-built)

shillings and pence sense

shiny and bright all right

shout and holler a collar

shovel and pick prison (slang **nick**)

shovels and spades AIDS

silver and gold old

skein of thread 1 bed 2 loaf of bread

skin and blister sister

sky rocket pocket

slip in the gutter butter

slug and snail fingernail

smack in the eye a pie

smash and grab taxi (**cab**)

smear and smudge a judge

snake in the grass **1** mirror (looking glass)
   2 drinking glass

snow and ice a price

soap and lather father

soap and water daughter

soapy bubble trouble

Sodom and Gomorrah to borrow (the biblical
   Cities of the Plain, destroyed by God for their
   wickedness [Genesis 19])

Southend Pier ear (at the English seaside resort
   of Southend-on-Sea, Essex)

Spanish Main a drain

spark and smoulder shoulder

spare rib a lie (informal **fib**)

spotted dick sick

stammer and stutter butter

stand at ease 1 cheese **2** fleas

Starsky and Hutch groin (**crotch**) (freelance detectives in the 1970s US TV series of that name)

Steffi Graf a laugh (German champion tennis player [b. 1969])

Steve McQueens jeans (Steve McQueen, US film star [1930-80])

Stewart Granger danger (British-born film actor [1913-93])

stick of rock penis (vulgar slang **cock**)

sticks and stones bones

stocks and shares stairs

Stoke-on-Trent homosexual (slang **bent**)

stop and go toe

stop and start heart

storm and strife wife

strange 'n' weird beard

struggle and strain **1** a train **2** to train

struggle and strife wife

sugar and honey money

sugar and spice **1** nice **2** ice

sunny south mouth

Suzie Wong a smell (slang **pong**) (from the film
  The World of Suzie Wong [1960], based on the
  novel by Richard Mason [1919-97])

swallow and sigh collar and tie

swear and cuss (curse) bus

Sylvester Stallone alone (US film star [b.
  1946])

syrup, syrup of figs wig

Tt

taxi rank bank (financial)

tea leaf thief

tent peg leg

Terry Waite late [British religious adviser held
   hostage in the Lebanon while negotiating the
   release of other hostages [b. 1939])

there first a thirst

these and those clothes

thick and thin **1** a chin **2** gin **3** a grin

this and that **1** cat **2** hat **3** bat (cricket)

throw me in the dirt shirt

tickle your fancy male homosexual (slang **nancy**)

Tilbury Docks **1** socks **2** venereal disease (informal **pox**)

tin flute a suit

tin of beans jeans

tin tack dismissal from a job (informal **the sack**)

tin tacks facts

titfer, tit for tat hat

tit willow a pillow

to and fro snow

tod, Tod Sloane, on one's alone, on one's own

toilet roll dole (unemployment benefit)

tom, tomfoolery jewellery

Tom and Dick sick

tomato purée jury

Tom Mix **1** fix, predicament **2** six (US film actor, star of over 400 Westerns [1880-1940])

tommy guns diarrhoea (informal **the runs**) (from the Thompson submachine-gun, used by US gangsters and by the Allies during the Second World War)

Tommy Steele eel (stage name of Thomas Hicks, British pop singer and actor [b. 1936])

Tom Sawyer lawyer (hero of the novel [1876] of the same name by the US writer Mark Twain [Samuel Langhorne Clemens; 1835-1910])

Tony Benn ten pounds sterling (British Labour politician [b. 1925])

Tony Blair hair (British Labour politician [b. 1953]; Prime Minister [1997-])

top hat **1** a chat **2** rat **3** fool (informal **prat**)

Tower Bridge refrigerator (informal **fridge**) (famous landmark and tourist attraction spanning the Thames in London)

town crier liar

Trafalgar Square chair (Central London
    landmark named after the British naval victory
    over the French at Trafalgar [1805])

trolley and tram ham

trouble and strife **1** wife **2** life

troubles and cares stairs

Turkish bath a laugh

twist and twirl girl

two and eight nervous state

two-bob bit bowel movement (vulgar slang **shit**)

two-by-four prostitute (**whore**)

two eyes of blue! too true!

two-thirty dirty

Uu

ugly sister a blister

umbrella man, boyfriend (informal **fella**)

Uncle Bert shirt

Uncle Billy chilly

Uncle Ned **1** head **2** bed

Uncle Reg vegetables (informal **veg**)

up and under thunder

up a tree three

Vv

Vanity Fair chair (title of a novel [1848] by the English novelist William Makepeace Thackeray [1811-63]; the phrase comes from the allegory *A Pilgrim's Progress* [1678] by the English writer and preacher John Bunyan [1628-88])

Vera Lynn **1** gin **2** skin (Dame Vera Lynn, stage name of the British singer Vera Lewis [b. 1917], known as 'the Forces' Sweetheart' during the Second World War)

Vincent Price ice (US film star [1911-93])

Ww

Wallace and Gromit vomit (animated plasticine film characters created in the 1980s)

watch and chain brain

water hen ten

weasel and stoat coat

weeping willow pillow

Westminster Abbey taxi driver (informal
   cabbie) (famous Gothic church and tourist
   attraction in London)

whistle, whistle and flute a suit

White Cliffs of Dover over, finished

wick, Hampton Wick penis (vulgar slang
   prick) (village in Greater London)

wicked rumours women's knickers (informal
   bloomers)

Widow Twankey 1 handkerchief (informal
   hanky) **2** an American (slang **Yankee**) (comic
   character from the pantomime *Aladdin*)

William Tell a smell (early fourteenth-century
   semi-legendary Swiss patriot who reputedly
   shot an apple from his son's head with his
   crossbow)

wind and kite website

wooden plank an American (slang **Yank**)

woolly vest nuisance (**pest**)

working classes spectacles (**glasses**)

worry and strife wife

Wyatt Earp a belch (informal **burp**)
 (US lawman and gunfighter [1848-1929])

Yarmouth bloater car (informal **motor**)

yellow silk milk

Yorkshire tyke microphone (informal **mike**)
 (slang for someone from Yorkshire)

yours and ours flowers

Zz

Zane Grey wages (**pay**) (US writer of Westerns
[1875-1939])

ENGLISH

to

RHYMING

SLANG

Aa

advice lump of ice

AIDS shovels and spades

alcoholic (lush) comb and brush

all right harbour light; Isle of Wight; shiny and
bright

alone Darby and Joan; Jack Jones, on one's;
Sylvester Stallone; tod, Tod Sloane, on one's

American, Yank, Yankee board and plank;
ham shank; Sherman tank; Widow Twankey;
wooden plank

anus, arsehole, shitter Elephant and Castle;
Gary Glitter

arm burglar alarm; false alarm; lucky charm

army daft and barmy; Kate Carney

aunt garden plant

Bb

back Cilla Black; haystack; penny black; roof rack

bad jack the lad

bad breath king death

bail Royal Mail

baked beans kings and queens

balls, bollocks, knackers (testicles) cheese and crackers; cobblers, cobbler's awls; fun and frolics; Jackson Pollocks; Max Walls; Niagara Falls; orchestra stalls

bank (financial) Arthur Rank; cab rank; iron tank; rattle and clank; taxi rank

bar bazaar; jack tar

barrow bow and arrow

basin Charley Mason; Fortnum & Mason

basinful (a great deal) Charley Mason

bat (cricket) this and that

bath hat and scarf

beard strange 'n' weird

bed born and bred; skein of thread;
    Uncle Ned

beer Crimea; pig's ear

beer, pint of never fear

beers Britney Spears

belch Raquel Welch

believe Adam and Eve; Christmas Eve

bell hair gel

belly, stomach Auntie Nellie; Darby Kelly

bent, corrupt Clark Kent

berk, stupid person Berkeley Hunt; Charlie
   Smirke

bet, flutter give and get; grumble and mutter;
   house to let

bigot Lester Piggott

bike, bicycle clever Mike; do as you like; Iron
   Mike

bird (woman) lemon curd

bitter (beer), pint of Gary Glitter; giggle and
   titter; laugh and titter

blind bacon rind

blister brother and sister; ugly sister

boat frog in the throat; nanny goat

body hot toddy

bogey, snot old fogey

boil (spot) can of oil; Conan Doyle

bones sticks and stones

bonkers, crazy marbles and conkers

book Captain Cook

bookie, bookmaker cream cookie

boots daisy roots; King Canutes

borrow Sodom and Gomorrah

bottle Aristotle

bowel movement, dump Donald Trump

Boy Scout Brussels sprout

braces airs and graces; Epsom races

brain down the drain; watch and chain

brake (vehicle) Charlie Drake

brandy Charley Randy; fine and dandy;
    Mahatma Gandhi

bread needle and thread

break (free time) Charlie Drake

breast, titty Bristol, Bristol City; Mae West

breath life and death

bribe, bung Jimmy Young

brick Dublin trick

brothel flea and louse

brother one another

burp Wyatt Earp

burst Geoff Hurst

bus don't make a fuss; swear and cuss (curse)

butter Calcutta, cough and stutter; mutter and
  stutter; slip in the gutter; stammer and stutter

buttocks, arse, bum bubble gum; chorus and
  verse; fife and drum; kingdom come

button Len Hutton

Cc

cabbie (taxi driver) Westminster Abbey

cadge coat and badge

café Colonel Gaddafi

car, motor haddock and bloater; jam jar;
la-di-dah; rattle and jar; Yarmouth bloater

car crash sausage and mash

cash, readies bangers and mash; dot and dash;
Nelson Eddies; pie and mash; sausage and
mash

cat this and that

chair here and there; Lionel Blair; Trafalgar
Square; Vanity Fair

chalk (used in billiards) Duke of York;
Lambeth Walk

chance Charles Dance

change (money) rifle range

charabanc (coach) bow and arrow

chat top hat

cheat daisy beat

cheek hide and seek

cheese bended knees; cough and sneeze; flying trapeze; John Cleese; stand at ease

cheque chicken's neck; goose's neck; Gregory Peck; nervous wreck; pain in the neck

chief prison officer corned beef

child, kid, nipper dustbin lid; fly-tipper; God forbid; saucepan lid

chill frock and frill

chilly Uncle Billy

chin Errol Flynn; thick and thin

chip(s) Jagger's lips; jockey's whip

chum, friend finger and thumb

church seek and search

cider runner and rider

cigar la-di-dah

cigarette, fag oily rag; old nag; Oxford bag; puff
and drag

cigarette lighter kung-fu fighter

cinema, pictures dolly mixtures

clever now and never

clothes these and those

clue, idea Danny La Rue; pot of glue

coal merry old soul

coat billy goat; nanny goat; pound note; weasel
and stoat

cocaine, coke big bloke

cocoa Orinoco

cold brave and bold; Cheltenham gold

collar shout and holler

collar and tie swallow and sigh

comb garden gnome; ideal home

committed for trial over the stile

concertina constant screamer

cough Darren Gough; on and off

cousin baker's dozen

coward Charley Howard

cramp rising damp

crook babbling brook

cupboard Mother Hubbard

curry Ruby Murray

Dd

daft fore and aft

dance kick and prance

danger Stewart Granger

daughter bottle of porter; bottle of water; bricks
and mortar; soap and water

dead brown bread; buttered bread; currant
bread; gone to bed; potted head

deaf Mutt and Jeff; pudding chef

degree (university), first-class Geoff Hurst

degree (university), lower-second (2:2)
Desmond

degree (university), third-class Douglas
Hurd

detective, dick club and stick

diarrhoea, runs tommy guns

diet peace and quiet

dinner Charley Skinner; Jimmy Skinner; Michael Winner; saint and sinner

dirty two-thirty

disappear Brighton Pier

dish Lillian Gish

doddle (something simple) Glenn Hoddle

dog London fog

dole (unemployment benefit) cob o'coal; jam roll; Nat King Cole; Old King Cole; rock'n'roll; sausage roll; toilet roll

door Rory O'Moore

door-to-door salesman forty-four

dope (cannabis) bar of soap; Bob Hope

dough (money) cod's roe

drain Spanish Main

dress more or less

drill Benny Hill

drink, booze kitchen sink; pick and choose;
River Ouse

dripping (fat) Doctor Crippen

drum finger and thumb

drunk, blotto, pissed, plastered booed and
hissed; Brahms and Liszt; elephant's trunk;
hand and fist; lord and mastered; Oliver Twist;
Santa's grotto

Ee

ear bottle of beer; glass of beer; King Lear;
Southend Pier

earner (profit-making scheme) Bunsen
burner

easy ham and cheesy

eel Tommy Steele

egg borrow and beg

eight garden gate; Harry Tate

e-mail British Rail

employer, master lath and plaster

erection general election

everywhere round and square

excrement/excrete, shit, turd Douglas Hurd;
    Eartha Kitt; lemon curd; two-bob bit

exhausted, knackered Christmas crackered;
    cream crackered

eyes minces, mince pies; puddings and pies

face(s) airs and graces; Chevy Chase; deuce and
    ace; Epsom races; kipper and plaice

facts brass tacks; tin tacks

fake Sexton Blake

fanny (vagina) Orphan Annie

fare (transport) grey mare

fart apple tart; broken heart; D'Oyly Carte; horse
    and cart; Lionel Bart; raspberry tart

father soap and lather

favour Cheesey Quaver

feet dog's, dog's meat; plates, plates of meat

fight left and right; read and write

file (tool) Plymouth Argyll

fine (penalty) bottle of wine; Calvin Klein

fingernail slug and snail

fingers bell-ringers

fire Jeremiah; Molly McGuire

fish Lillian Gish

five Jack's alive; Lady Godiva; man alive

five pounds, fiver deep-sea diver; Lady Godiva

fix (predicament) Tom Mix

flares (flared trousers) Lionel Blairs

flea(s) Jennie Lee; Nancy Lee; stand at ease

flight (escape) read and write

floor Rory O'Moore

flower(s) happy hour; yours and ours

flu inky blue

food in the mood; in the nude

fool, chump, dope Joe Soap; lump and bump

fork Duke of York; roast pork

four door-to-door; knock at the door; open the door

fox Charles James

fridge Tower Bridge

fuck, ride, shag goose and duck; Joe McBride; lame duck; Melvyn Bragg; rubber duck

Gg

gaol ginger ale; jug and pail; moan and wail; rusty nail

garden beg your pardon; Dolly Varden

ghost pillar and post

gin Brian O'Flynn; needle and pin; nose and chin; thick and thin; Vera Lynn

gin and tonic philharmonic

girl ivory pearl; ocean pearl; ribbon and curl; twist and twirl

give over! Chatham and Dover

glass (drinking) snake in the grass

glasses (spectacles) working classes

gold hot and cold

good Robin Hood

gout salmon and trout

gravy Royal Navy

Greek bubble and squeak

grin thick and thin

groin, crotch rabbit hutch, Starsky and Hutch

ground safe and sound

haemorrhoids, piles chalfonts, Chalfont St Giles; Farmer Giles; Nobby Stiles; Nuremberg trials

hair barnet, Barnet Fair; Tony Blair

half cow and calf

ham trolley and tram

hand(s) brass band; Ramsgate Sands

handkerchief, hanky Widow Twankey

hard bread and lard

hat, lid ball and bat; God forbid; hard and flat; lean
and fat; this and that; titfer, tit for tat

head ball of lead; cherry red; crust of bread; loaf,
loaf of bread; pound of lead; ruby red; Uncle Ned

head of the family daily bread

heart horse and cart; stop and start

hill Jack and Jill

hole merry old soul

home, place drum and bass; ham and bone

horse bottle of sauce; Charing Cross

horse races airs and graces

house cat and mouse; flea and louse; rat and mouse

huff (bad temper) cream puff

husband, man old pot and pan; pot and pan

ice sugar and spice; Vincent Price

jam baby's pram

jeans Steve McQueens; tin of beans

jelly Mother Kelly

Jesus Christ (in oaths) cheese and rice

jewellery tom, tomfoolery

job knocker and knob

joke can of Coke; egg yoke

judge Barnaby Rudge; smear and smudge

jury tomato purée

key(s) dancing fleas; Jennie Lee; knobbly knee

kipper Jack the Ripper

kiss hit and miss

knee(s) biscuits and cheese; Cecil Gee; chips and peas; high seas

knife charming wife; drum and fife; husband and wife; man and wife

LI

ladies' toilet Rosie O'Grady's

lark (bird, prank) Noah's ark

late Harry Tate; Terry Waite

laugh bubble bath; cow and calf; giraffe; Steffi Graf; Turkish bath

lawyer Tom Sawyer

lazy Gert and Daisy

lazy person, skiver backseat driver

leg(s) bacon and eggs; clothes pegs; Dutch pegs; Easter egg; Mystic Meg; Scotch eggs; tent peg

letter Henrietta

liar Dunlop tyre; town crier

lie, fib collar and tie; spare rib

life fork and knife; trouble and strife

light Isle of Wight

liver bow and quiver; broken quiver

loaf of bread skein of thread

lodger artful dodger; Jolly Roger

lodgings, digs Ronnie Biggs

look butcher's, butcher's hook; Captain Cook

lorry sad and sorry

love heavens above

Mm

magistrate garden gate

mail, post Holy Ghost; Jimmy Nail

man, boyfriend, fella umbrella

mare Lionel Blair

margarine little and large

married cash and carried

marry dot and carry

masturbate, wank Arthur Rank; Jodrell Bank

masturbator, wanker merchant banker

match itch and scratch

mate, friend china, china plate; Dutch, Dutch plate; garden gate

mean, tight inside right; Isle of Wight

meeting Buster Keaton

meter (gas, electricity, etc.) Little Peter

microphone, mike Yorkshire tyke

milk satin and silk; yellow silk

minute (time) cock linnet

mirror, looking glass snake in the grass

money bees and honey; bread and honey; Bugs
   Bunny; Easter bunny; pot of honey; sugar and
   honey

moody Punch and Judy

mother one another

mouth east and south; north and south; sunny
   south

muddle kiss and cuddle

mum (keep quiet) finger and thumb

murder iron girder

Nn

nag, scold paper bag

nark, police informer car park; Hyde Park;
  Noah's ark

neck bushel and peck; Gregory Peck

nerve, courage bottle, bottle and glass

nervous state two and eight

nice chicken and rice; sugar and spice

nicker (pound sterling) cherrypicker

nine Calvin Klein

nipple raspberry ripple

no Brown Joe

nonsense, rubbish cobblers, cobbler's awls

nose, snout salmon and trout

nuisance, pest woolly vest

Oo

off (stale) Frank Bough

old silver and gold

one (number) buttered bun

onions corns and bunions

over, finished White Cliffs of Dover

own, to be on one's on one's Jack Jones

Pp

pain Michael Caine; Petticoat Lane

pants, bloomers, knickers Alan Whickers;
 Brenda Frickers; wicked rumours

park Noah's ark

parole jam roll

parrot Jasper Carrott

party gay and hearty; hale and hearty

peep, look Bo Peep

penis, cock, dick, pecker, prick Black &
 Decker; bob and dick; Mars and Venus; stick of
 rock; wick, hampton, Hampton Wick

penniless, broke, skint Bernie Flint; boracic;
 boracic lint; heart of oak; pink lint

penny Abergavenny

pepper high-stepper

person, geezer fridge freezer; ice-cream freezer

piano Joanna

pickles Harvey Nichols

pie Captain Bligh; smack in the eye

pill Damon Hill; Jack and Jill; Jimmy Hill

pillow rolling billow; tit willow; weeping willow

plate Harry Tate; pearly gate

play night and day

please hairy knees

pocket chain and locket; Davy Crockett; penny
  locket; sky rocket

poker Orinoco

police officer, cop, copper bottle and stopper;
  ginger pop; pork chop

ponce, pimp Charlie Ronce

pong, smell Hong Kong; Suzie Wong

pony (twenty-five pounds) macaroni

pork Duke of York

port (wine) didn't ought

post (at a racecourse) Holy Ghost

pox, venereal disease boots and socks; cardboard box; Tilbury Docks

pram jar of jam

prat, fool paper hat; top hat

price snow and ice

priest bag of yeast

prison, nick cow's lick; shovel and pick

prison cell flowery dell

prostitute, whore boat and oar; forty-four; Rory O'Moore; two-by-four

pub, boozer battle cruiser; nuclear sub; rub-a-dub

publican, mine host dripping toast

pudding basin Fortnum and Mason

punter Billy Bunter

purse doctor and nurse

Qq

queer (homosexual), bent, fairy, gay, nancy bottle of scent; Brighton Pier; Duke of Kent; ginger beer; Howard's Way; Julian Clary; King Lear; Milky Way; Stoke-on-Trent; tickle your fancy

queer (strange) ginger beer

queue pot of glue

Rr

rain, shower bag of flour; David Gower; Eiffel
Tower; France and Spain; happy hour

randy Mahatma Gandhi; port and brandy

rat top hat

razor House of Fraser

rent Burton-on-Trent; Duke of Kent

ride Charlie Pride

right (side) Isle of Wight

ring Highland fling

road frog and toad

rotten Dolly Cotton

rough Brian Clough

round (of drinks) hare and hound

row, quarrel bull and cow

rum finger and thumb; kingdom come

run away, go scarper, Scapa Flow

Ss

sack (dismissal) tin tack

sale Jimmy Nail

scar Mars Bar

sense pounds and pence; shillings and pence

seven God in heaven

sex Oedipus Rex

sexual intercourse, ride Joe McBride

shandy Mahatma Gandhi

shark Noah's ark

shave dig a grave; ocean wave

shirt throw me in the dirt; Uncle Bert

shoes rhythm and blues

shoulder(s) rocks and boulders; spark and
    smoulder

showy, flash pie and mash

sick bob and dick; Moby Dick; Pat and Mick;
    spotted dick; Tom and Dick

silly Piccadilly

sing Highland fling

sister skin and blister

six chopping sticks; pick up sticks; Tom Mix

sixty-six clickety-click

skin Vera Lynn

sky shepherd's pie

slap brandy snap

sleep, kip Bo Peep; jockey's whip

slipper(s) big dippers; Jack the Ripper

smell heaven and hell; William Tell

smoke (cigarettes, etc.) cough and choke; Joe
Roke; laugh and joke

snake Joe Blake

sneeze breed and cheese

snore lion's roar; rain and pour

snow to and fro

snuff (tobacco) blindman's buff

soap Band of Hope; frisk and frolic

socks Tilbury Docks

son bath bun; Chelsea bun; currant bun

soup loop the loop

sparrow bow and arrow

spoon blue moon; Lorna Doone

squatter pig's trotter

squeal, inform on someone conger eel

stain Michael Caine

stairs apples, apples and pears; stocks and shares;
    troubles and cares

stale Jimmy Nail

starving Hank Marvin; Lee Marvin

station (railway) poor relation

steak Joe Blake

steal, pinch half-inch

stench Judi Dench

stink pen and ink

stinking Abraham Lincoln

stocking reeling and rocking

story Jackanory

stout (beer) salmon and trout

strangers Queen's Park Rangers

string Highland fling

stripper (striptease artiste) herring and
  kipper

suit bag of fruit; fiddle and flute; tin flute;
  whistle, whistle and flute

suitcase crowded space

sun bath bun; Chelsea bun; currant bun; hit and
  run

sunglasses, shades jack of spades

swear (curse) lord mayor; rip and tear

Tt

table Betty Grable; Cain and Abel

talk ball of chalk; Duke of York

talker, informer Johnnie Walker

tan (colour) Peter Pan

taxi, cab flounder and dab; Joe Baxi; smash and grab

tea glory be; Gypsy Rose Lee; Jennie Lee; Nancy Lee; rosie, Rosie Lee

teeth Bexleyheath; Hampstead Heath; roast beef

telephone, phone Darby and Joan; dog and
bone; eau de cologne; ham and bone; Mike
Malone; Sharon Stone

television, telly custard and jelly; Mother Kelly

ten Big Ben; cock and hen, cockle and hen; water
hen

ten pounds, tenner Ayrton Senna; Big Ben;
cock and hen, cockle and hen; Tony Benn

theatre box Charles James

thief corned beef; leg of beef; tea leaf

thin needle and pin

thirst Geoff Hurst; there first

thirty Burlington Bertie

three up a tree

throat nanny goat

thunder up and under

ticket bat and wicket

tie (neckwear) Peckham Rye

tights fly-by-nights

till (cash) Benny Hill; Jack and Jill

time (prison sentence) bird, birdlime; grease and grime

toast Holy Ghost

toaster roller coaster

tobacco, snout salmon and trout

toe(s) buttons and bows; Sebastian Coe; stop and go

toilet, bog captain's log

tomato sauce dead horse

tongue Jimmy Young

too true! two eyes of blue!

tools crown jewels

tote (betting system) canal boat; nanny goat

tout salmon and trout

town Joe Brown

traffic warden Gay Gordon

train John Wayne; struggle and strain

train, to struggle and strain

trainer (shoe) Claire Rayner

tram jar of jam

tramp hurricane lamp; paraffin lamp

transport, wheels jellied eels

trouble soapy bubble

trousers, pants fleas and ants; insects and ants;
  round the houses

trowel Baden-Powell

true Irish stew

truth Maud and Ruth

twelve, dozen country cousin; monkey's cousin

twenty horn of plenty

twins needles and pins

tyre Billy Liar

umbrella Auntie Ella

Underground (London), Tube Oxo cube

understand, twig earwig

urine/urinate/urination, leak, pee, piddle, pish/piss, slash bangers and mash; bubble and squeak; Christopher Lee; gypsy's kiss; hit and miss; Jimmy Riddle; Leslie Ash; Lillian Gish; Pat Cash; pie and mash

Vv

van Peter Pan

vegetables, veg Uncle Reg

vest east and west

vicar pie and liquor

villain Harold Macmillan

vomit Wallace and Gromit

Ww

wad (roll of banknotes) Ken Dodd

wager John Major

wages, pay greengages; rock of ages; Zane Grey

waistcoat Charlie Prescott

waiter cheese grater; cold potato

walk ball of chalk; Duke of York

water didn't oughter; dirty daughter; fisherman's daughter; miller's daughter

website wind and kite

week bubble and squeak

whiskers hammer and discus

whisky, Scotch Charley Frisky; gay and frisky; gold watch

wife, missus bread knife; carving knife; drum and fife; Duchess of Fife; fork and knife; hugs and kisses; joy of my life; kiss of life; love and kisses; storm and strife; struggle and strife; trouble and strife; worry and strife

wig(s) guinea pig; Irish jig; syrup, syrup of figs

win nose and chin

wind (flatulence) Jenny Lind

window burnt cinder

wine Calvin Klein; River Tyne

winner hot dinner

wish plate and dish

word dicky-bird; early bird

wrong Hong Kong

Yy

yes Brown Bess

yuppie Hush Puppy